HOPE THROAT
Talk Talk Die

Poems written between 2022 - 2025
by Talk Talk Die / Benita Milner.
for Little Sword.

Copyright © 2025 Talk Talk Die

All rights reserved. No part of this book may be reprinted or reproduced or utilised in any form or by any electronic, mechanical, or other means, now known or hereafter invented, including photocopying and recording, or in any information storage or retrieval system, without permission in writing from the publisher.

Paperback 978-1-7640782-6-9

First published in 2025

Moonrise
Wonnarua and Gubbi Gubbi Country, Australia
www.moonrise.revolutionaries.com.au

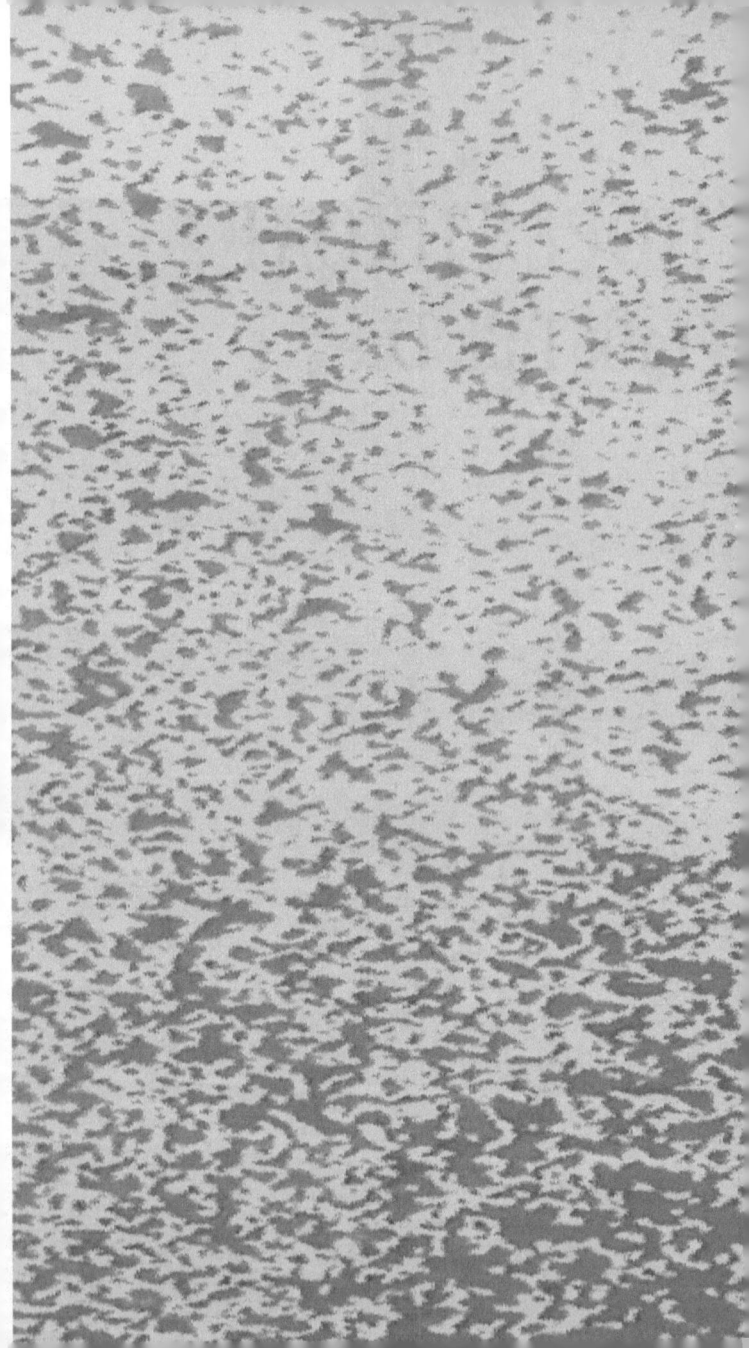

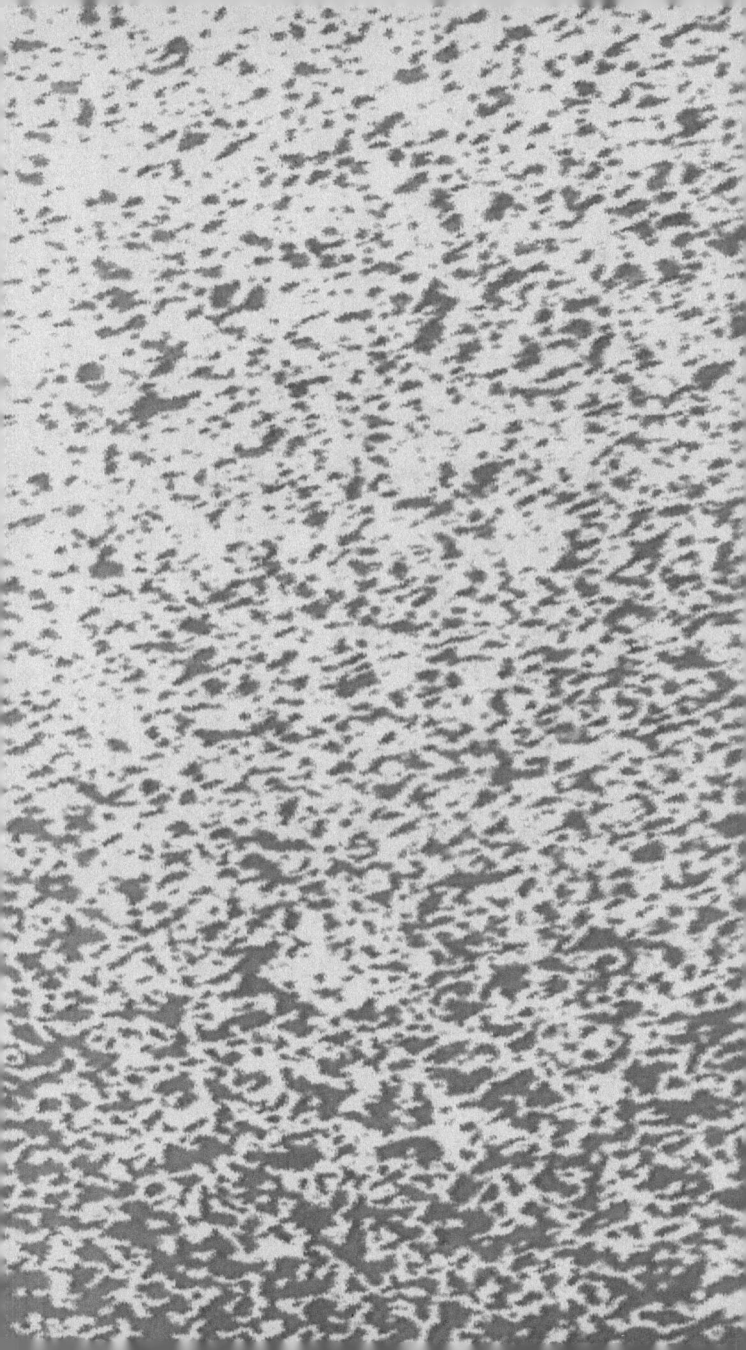

SORRY TO MY BODY.
I CANNOT CARRY TODAY.
THE PAINS OF HAVE TO AND MUST
ARE BEAUTIFUL AND LONG.

A WHOLE LIFE'S LIFTING
IS WAVING THROUGH LOVE,
DEVOTION OF CELLS,
A SIGNING OF SKIN
AND GIFTING OF AGE.

I TAKE IT TOO.
I TAKE THE HOURS AND
WILL.
I GIVE UP WHAT I CANNOT
KNOW IS GONE.
I LIVE IN THE DELIGHTS
AND DEATHS KNOWN TO ME.

ATOMS SEPERATING WITH EASE
KISSING OFF INTO EARTH.
LOVING PULSES FLOAT
AND SINK.

FLIPPING LIKE A SHINY COIN
THAT LANDS LIGHTHY
ON GRAVES.
ON HEADS
ON TAILS.
TRUSTED AND FAILING.

WALLOW LOVE
IN THIN WATER
KISSING GRAVEL
UNDER SUN.

SMALL FINGERS WANTING,
STRETCHING.
KNOWING THAT PLACE SO RIPE.
A WHOLE WORLD OF LIVING
LOST ON WHIM.

WRITE LETTERS
SO PIECES OF YOU
GET THERE
AHEAD OF BODY AND SOUL.

A PEACE GIFT YOU GOT
WADING IN MUD,
NOW UNWRAPPING
BETWEEN LAP AND KNEES.
A GUT-NAVEL JEWEL
ROLLING ROUND TONGUE.
SLIPPING AND DISPERSING
THROUGH FLESHY LAYERS
OF HARD HIGH ▬▬▬
AIRFUL SIGHS
FLOODING OUT.

DESPISE AND DISCOVER
AN UNENDING PLACE
OF RESISTANCE
AND GIVING IN.

LAYING ON LONG SPINE,
RESTING
IN TIGHT WHITE SKIN.

BODY SWALLOWS AGAIN
AND AGAIN,
THE OUTER FIRES
INGESTED UNTAMED.
ALL SHADES OF HEAT
COMPOSTING WITHIN.
AND SO ON
AND SO ROT.

PLATEAU FLAT.
WITH A WAITING SUIT
THICK IN THOUGHT.
HAULED ALONG
IN FULL DRESS
AS WATER CHOPS AND PULLS.
SOAKED AND DRIED

PLACED ASHORE,
NOW DEEP.
A PELTING BREATH
AS LIPS GRIP
ABOVE POUNDING
SALT AND SEA.

MIDDLE TO MIDDLE.
A MAGNET FOR IT.
MY SANDY SINK BODY
KISSING FUNNEL WALLS
TOWARDS IT.

SPACE SO FILLING
PUSHES AIR.
GRAVITYS DESTINY SMIRKS.

I CANNOT LIE ABOUT IT.
I LOATHE AND LOVE
IT HERE.

MOVEABLE AND IMOVABLE
OBJECTS ARRANGING
IN PATTERNS AND MODES.
INTERCHAGING,
WATER
ROCK
AIR
DIRT.

IMPATIENCE WAITING
FOR EASE
FOR A CHANCE TO
PUSH BODY ASIDE
FOR A REASON
TO FOLD DOWN SPIRIT.

FORGOTTEN FIRES BURNING.
BELOW ALL MOTIONS
OF PROFESSED DEFEAT.

A body waste
that stumbles
across gravels,
waking lawns.

Gridded lifeless
subdued suburbs
contorting twisting cube.

Rocket legs
run crooked.
Say home
say lead
say now.

CEROMONIOUS EULOGIES
AND LEAVING EMBRYOS
REPEAT IN LINES.

THRASHING BECOMES A
MARK ON ME.
AND I HOLD ITS RAISED
DENT ON MY ARM
LIKE A CHILD.

SICK WITH EXPANSION.
SKIN IS ONLY NOISE.
STRETCHED OUT TO TINY SQUARES
THAT ROAR
QUIETLY UNDER EVERYTHING.

STICKING TO EVERYTHING.
GLUEY HEART HANDS
TAKING ALL THERE IS
TO TAKE.

WILD SIDE OPENING.
SURROUNDED AS WE ARE.
FLOATING IN ~~████~~
FLIMSY PIECES.
I SEE HOW PEELED WE ARE,
HOW BENT INTO A SHAPE WE ARE.

SAD WISHING EYES CLOSE.
GLUEY LIDS STAY SHUT,
TAKING ALL THERE IS
TO TAKE.

POINTLESS BLUR POINTING.
TELLING ~~████~~ CALLING WORDS
THAT BOTHER TO COME
TO MIND.

~~████████~~ WAKING AND
STANDING WITH EFFORT.
DREAMING AND FIGHTING
IN EASE.

TICK OVER RISING REVULSIONS
AND SCORES.
MAKING PURPOSE OF
SCRAP THOUGHT
AND QUIET.

A HOLE MADE
IS A GAPE
THAT WIDENS
TIL DEATH.

SHAKING GLORIOUS.
MOVING
QUIET AND SLOW
OVER BUMPS
OVER WAVES.

RISING CLOTH
COMING UP
OVER THE YARD.
MANY HANDS
GUIDING ITS FORM TO THE GROUND.

AIR EXPELLS SOULS
IN ALL DIRECTIONS.
SUN LOCKS ONTO FLECKS
OF PEACE
AS ACHING CELLS GIVE IN
TO BREATHE OUT.

Asking and aching.
Little metal
under tongue.
The work of
many muscles
holding it there.

The crispness of mind
that keeps,
whispers in.

I press gently
I rock
I sway
between us.

CONDITIONLESS
BOUNDING
I GO.

PUSHED INTO
POWDER PALE BLUES
NEVER KNOWN.
ONLY REACHED
AND HELD THE MORE CLOSE
FOR THE SWINGING
HEAT SURROUNDING.

ITS SO SIMPLE
THIS DESIRE.
IT STARTS WITH A
BEAUTIFUL CHAIR,
FREE AND WILLING
THAT I SIT
AND WEEP IN IT.
THEN GOES
WILD AND FLOODED
UNFINISHED
TELLING AND UNTOLD.

PIECES ALL SURROUNDING
IN CIRCULAR CONSTELLATIONS
MOVING AND RULING.
LIGHT IS LESS.
WITH LESS MEMORY FOR TIME.

I AM CLOSE TO NOTHING
CLOSING ON EVERYTHING.

REACHING IN,
THERE IS NOTHING ELSE
TO DO.

MORE,
A CRACK OPENING INTO A CREVICE.
WE WILL GIVE IT MORE TIME.

A WINDOW FLEW OPEN.
GASPING, I'LL TAKE THAT AIR, I SAID.
THEN I TURNED
AND LEAPT
RIGHT THROUGH IT.

FOLLOW ON
GUIDED DARK.
~~FINGER~~ FINGER SKIN
HUGS INSIDE GROOVES.
~~COLLECTIONS~~ COLLECTIONS
COME ALONG WITH ME.
EVERY HUNG BACK PIECE
STRETCHES OUT.
SHADOW FEET,
ARMS MINE
AND YOURS.
COOL AIR RUSHING US.
SWEET DEATH
PURGING,
RETURNING US.

THIS DEEP IS SO.
AS WE LIVE
ON ONE ANOTHER. BOTH.
THE ISLAND
AND THE SKY.
THE DARK BLUE
AND THE SHIP.

UNCOMFORT
ACHING SKIN.
WE HAVE MADE A SORE PLACE
TO SLEEP
THAT DOES NOT GO AWAY.

RUNNING OVER CRACKS
HELD UP
TO PRESS DOWN
ON AIR
ESCAPING.

COME TO THIS
POINTED PLACE.
SLOPE-WHIP UP,
FIND AIR.

STILL RISING
AT WEIGHT
AND GOOD STEAD.

ALL HEAVY BURDENS
WAKING UP TO GREET
THE MORNING.
TIME IS LOVING
AND TIME IS SOUR.

MY MOTHER WAS HERE.
I CAN SMELL HER PERFUME
IN MY BABYS HAIR.
THE DOLLS ARE LINED UP.
~~████~~ COMPANIONS
CONVERSATIONS
PICNICS
TEA PARTIES
TO THE SHOP
THE BEACH.

KITCHEN TOPS ARE
CLEAR AND SMOOTH AND DRY.
MY MOTHER LINGERS.
MY CHILD SWINGS ON
~~████~~ MY LEGS,
~~████~~ RINGS A ROSIE KITCHEN ANKLE.
THE HOUSE IS JUST HOW IT
SHOULD BE.

PADDED WELL.
ALL AROUND THE BODY
INTO THE MOUTH.
A SWELLING SAFETY
THAT CHAFES.

HERE IN HEAVENLY HELL.
CONTORTING ALL LIMBS
FOR PIECES OF A MIND
DRIVEN WRECKLESS.
WRACKED
WITH UNKNOWNS.

I REMEMBER HEART OF GOLD.
SOFT SPINNING
WHERE THE SIDES
WERE MORE LENGTHS
THAN LIMBS.
CLOSED SPECKLED EYES
ONLY DREAMING
AND SEEING SUN.
LEAPING HARDER,
A BONE OVER A BONE.
NOTHING LEAVES,
~~~~ NOTHING COMES.

LOST HOT QUICK SILVER.
DAY BURNING.
IN A RIPE MIND
WAKING UP DONE.
TURNING BACK DOWN,
DOWN INTO ASH PILLOW,
INTO SORRYS CIRCLE.
I WILL NOT RISE.
I WILL NOT RISE.
BENDING ANY WAY THERE IS,
OUT OF LINES
AND REASONS.
OUT OF TRACKS THAT GO
ON FOREVER
THROUGH ANY PAIN
THAT COULD CAPITAL COME.
NO DEATH,
NO WIDE WORLD DEATH
OR DEAD SUN
COULD STOP IT.
THE WHEELS OIL NICELY
WHILE EVERYTHING ENDS.

ENDINGS IN ABUNDANCE.
I CUT THE TOE
TO GIVE IN.
THERE IS NO CURSE
IN THIS TUNNEL.
IT IS THE DIRT THAT
MOUNDS IN TIME.
CLEARING
AND COMPACTING,
BREATHING AND
UNFOLDING
WITH THE GROUND WE PUSH
~~━━━━━━━~~ AND REST ON.

PAIN PIN DRAGGING.
LETTING LISTS GROW AND RUN.
TOTAL FIRE BURNING
ONE SORRY FLAME.
ONE WITHOUT FORGIVNESS.
~~ONE~~ ONE MORE
IS TOO MUCH.

FLAGELLATING STRAW.
~~~~ LOADLESS
UNDER ONE EYE.
CONDEMNING CHORUS
FOR SOME.
WEIGHTLESS WORDS
WEIGHING
MORE MORE.
MORE IS TOO MUCH.

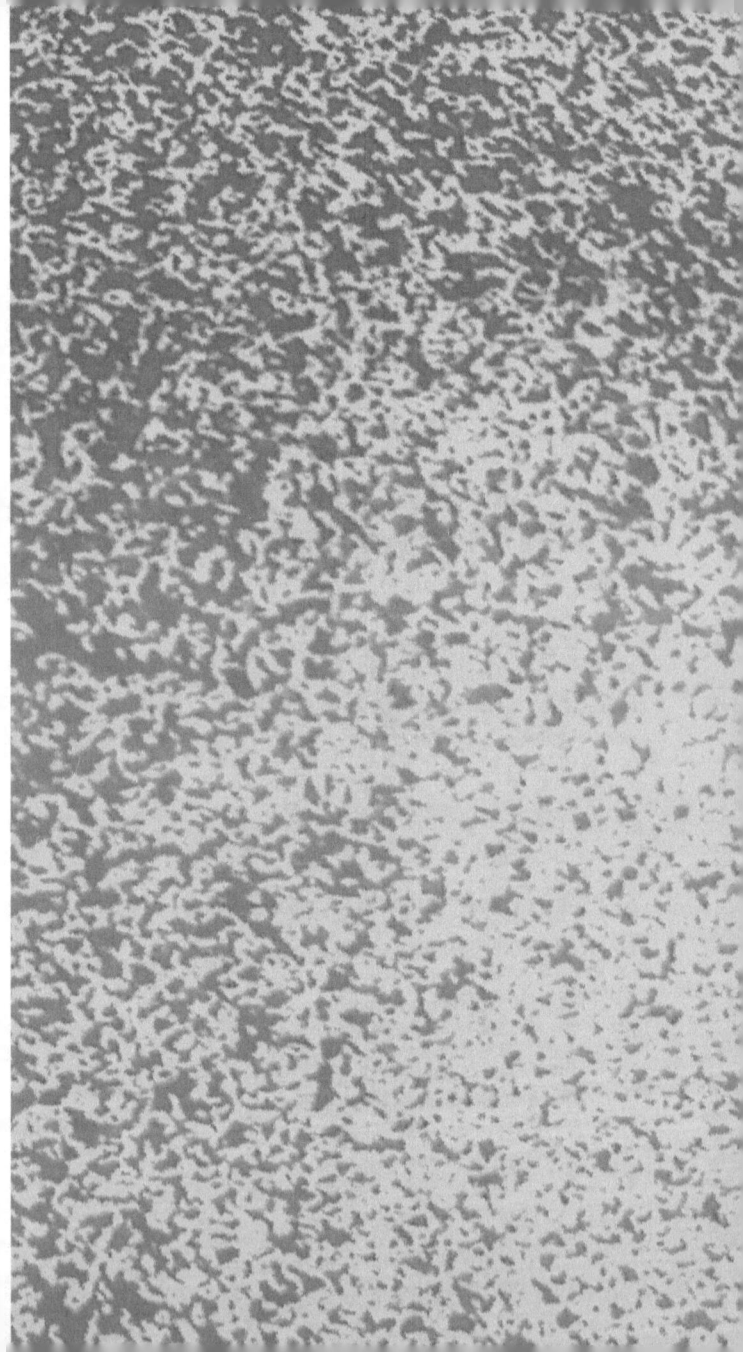

LAST BLOOD
CRAWLING DRY OUT.
TAKING WRENCHING TIME
WITH FLAKES SHIFTING.

LAST BLOOD LAST.
COULD PARTS OF THIS SOUL
SETTLE
TO BREAK FOR NEW SKIN
AND STARS.
FUZZING ECHOS IMPRINTING LOVE.
RUNNING OFF SIDES
STRETCHING OUT TO
A TINY BEATING HEART.

■ BETWEEN THE HOUSE
AND THE YARD
I SLIP AWAY.

SPLIT LIGHT
PATCH WORKING.
TAKING NEW FORMS
AS I MORPH
AROUND THE NIGHT.
HOPING,
RUFFLING THROUGH SKYLINES
AND QUIET DRAWS.

EVERY NIGHT LEADS
TO MORNING.
I TASTE SHADOW
I SEE SUN.

COASTING FLAME
LIVING ASIDE SELF
SO LONG.
IN SACRIFICIAL LOVE.
CIRCLES OF
NIGHT AND DAY.

Love rubbed on rock
and bone.
Its changing form
weighing at the feet
of mountains.

So long is this earth-wave
of touching.
Two souls ever undulating.
Sandy flecks floating
in every pocket
where we sink hands.

Proud eternal marble,
nothing teaches like time
as lovers guard the stone.

SECOND SHELL OF MY BODY
MOVING BEYOND ME
IN SPEEDS AND BOLTS OF
MOMENTS.

GRAB AROUND THE NECK
NO.
UNDERARM. NO.
WAIST. NO.
NOT THERE. SHE'S NOT.

TURN TURNING HEAD.
I CAN ONLY SEE
IN CIRCLES
SPUN TO SICKNESS.

Clicked out.
A knee,
A shoulder,
Removed from its place.
Missing home
While sitting under the roof
Of that home.
At the table
Staring into the wood
To make the food come,
To make the room burn,
To reach wider
Than the melting walls
And the bathtub I scrub
For my landlord.

ONE SET OF RULES IS THIS,
YOU ARE DEAD, DYING, ROLLING
UPWARD, FLYING AND ▬▬▬
FUSING WITH DIRT.

CONVERGENCE OF
DEEP WATER MASSES
UPWELLING AND
DOWNWELLING.
WISHFUL FOR LAND,
FOR THE PERIOD OF DIRT.
TIME WHEN FEET
WERE LEVEL.
NOT PEDDLING WET ATOMS
IN VIOLENCE.

TENSILE STRENGTH
AND OUTWARD LIMITS.
PUT ON MORE.
SHE IS BENT AND BENDING
SHE IS CASTING THOUGHTS
OF FLAMES.
MAYBE A COMBUSTION
COULD SAVE. ~~━━━~~

HEAT LOADING CLOSER.
ENTROPY COMING OF AGE.
AN END FIT FOR
SLOW LONG BURNING
AT THE PYRE.
SHE LIKES DIRT,
VOLCANIC AND FERTILE.
SHE LIVES IN IT.
EXPELLING FLAMES
IN A PRAYER TO
OMIT AND COOL.

VOICES BACKGROUND-BEATING,
DEEP HOLLOW MEMORIES
OF LOSING TEARS.

BOTH CHEECKS SWEPT AT.
AFFECTION FOR THE TWO SIDES.

SWERVING FOR VISUAL,
MOMENTUM TAKES ON SCRAPS.
PIECES FLOODING
INTO SENTIMENT CENTRES
WHERE ALL OF IT IS HIDING.

MARKS TWIST ON TWO SOULS,
MORE SIMILAR IN SUFFERING
WE LAY.

STRONG PACE.
A RYTHM OF SHADES
AND HOOKS
PULL OVER.

UNRAVELLING MINDS MEET
IN COLOSSAL DARKNESS
WHERE HEAVY BEGINS.

FIGHTING THE STONE.
LOWER LOWER.
TAKING PLACE
IN UNDERNEATH.
THE LOVELY WEIGHT
REVOLTING
UNTIL
GLORY.

CROSSING A GOODBYE
OVER CHEST.
HANDS REACHING,
STRETCHING LANSCAPES
OF SOULS AND TIME.

OILED AND OILED
THE WHEEL SLIPS ON.

CORNERSTONE NAIL.
RED ON RUST,
A NOTE.
ALIVE ON SLEEPING.
THERE ON WAKING.
TRUSTING WEIGHT TO RISE.

UNDER TURNED ROCKS
MORE MESSAGES
INDENT IN DIRT.
STEADY AS AIR,
THERE'S FIRE TO FOLLOW.

LIFT ME IF YOU THINK
IM NOT TOO HEAVY.
IM HERE
HOLDING YOU
AND YOUR HAMMER TOO.

GOOD STAMINA
FOR THRESHOLD PAIN.
HANDS IN LONG GROOVES
ALONG ROCK,
LOCKING ELEMENT
TO ELEMENT.
DISTANCE COVERED
WITH STRONG GAZE.
PINNED TO A PLACE
INVISIBLE AND CALLING.

PUNCHED OFF AND
DOWN IN HOLE.
A COMPLETE PLACE.
TOUCHING BACK ON
THE FIRST LINE.

REMINISCE HOLE.
DARK ENOUGH FOR
SQUIRMING WORMS
UNRUBBED BY LONELY.

SHOULDER ROCK
CRACK THROAT.
HEAL UP CUTS
DO IT IN DIRT.
ON SIDE
LEGS RUNNING,
PUSHING DARK AROUND.
CRY CRY AND
GET OUT GOOD.

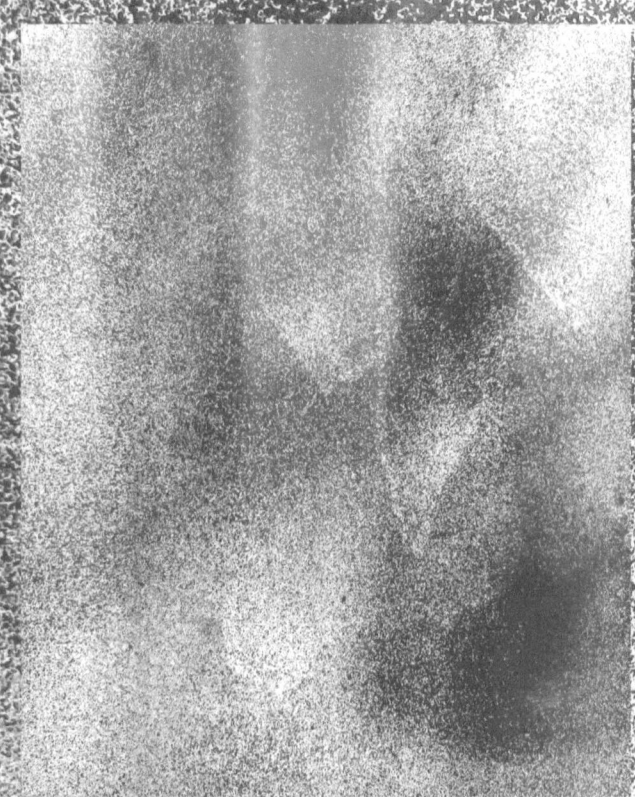

LINES OVERLAYING AND LAPPING.
FAST HARD TOUCHING
OF NON TOUCHING PIECES
UNTIL GONE.

GIVEN UP THUMPINGS
GROWN SOFTER
AND UNTREAD
UNTIL GONE.

CLAPPED CELLS TOGETHER
IN LIGHTENING LOVE.
LEAVING A WONDER
OF TIMES IMPRESSIONS
OF DEARNESS.
LIVING UNTIL GONE.

NOTHING LIKE NOTHING
HANGING IN A
PLACE THAT HELD
UNTIL GONE.

BANGED UP BLUR.
HOLD ONTO THE PEN
HOLD ONTO THE BABY,
THE GRATED MOMENTUM
THAT SWINGS
AND MAKES FIRE,
MAKES YOU.

HEAD COASTER BENDING
ON SLOW MOTION BENDS.
NO AMOUNTS OF
WHIP OR SHARP SLIP THROUGH.
YOU JUST DONT ABSORB
LIKE BEFORE.

I BITE ON EVERYTHING
TO KEEP ME HERE.
A TOKEN OF EXISTING.

CONFIDING MIND.
LOOKING HERE FOR
PIECES THAT STAY DOWN,
MATERIAL THAT TACKS
OR LETS WEIGHT
KEEP PRESSURE
FOR PEACE.

CRYING GUT.
TURNING PARTS
AROUND AROUND.
CIRCLING WHAT IS
CLEAR AND TRUE.
NUDGING INTO PLACE
BY PULLING BREATH,
SUCKING SIDES
TO FIT.

TICKING TONGUE
GAURDING THE TOO MUCH.
FLATTENING
TO FLESH FLOOR.
WHERE REASON
CAN COME SLOWLY TO.

PEARLY PLEASURE BELOW GROUND.
SURROUNDED BLUE,
A DEPTH OF
OIL FOR JOINTS.
A BIRTHRIGHT PLACE
CUT INTO.
OUT OF HOME
~~~~ HOLDING SIDES
FOR STRONG GROUND.
DREAMING FIRST
VOCATIONS OF AIR.

A MADNESS LEAVES MY BODY,
LEAVES ME LIGHTLY WEIGHING.
A SILENCE IS FILLED
WITH WHERE YOU HAVE GONE.

A BURST OF BEGINNING
ENDS SLOW.
WITH THICKNESS TO PUSH
SHINS THROUGH.

ATOP THE SILK WATER OF LOSS
YOU FLOAT.
I SWAY THAT I CAN STILL
TOUCH YOU THERE.

LOVE KILLS
THE NIGHT
AND BREAKS UP EARTH
WITH WAVES.
VIOLENT OCEANS
SICK ON JOY
ROCKING ▬▬ LOW.

LOVE KILLS
WEAPONS IN ME.
BLOCKING BLOWS
UNTIL ALL IS PUT DOWN.
▬▬ MUDDY HALF LEGS
AND HORSES LEFT OVER.

LOVE KILLS
THE DROWNING HOURS
OF TOO MUCH TRUTH
AND WORRY.
A QUIVERING LIMB
GIVING IN
TO BEING CAUGHT,
HELD, LIFTED AND
WARMED.

WEIGHT ON ONE SIDE
SWAYING TO TILT,
TO FORM
WITH THE OTHER.

LOWER BURNING
FIRST CIRCLE SWIRLING.
COMING UP ON AIR.

RILING TO RUMBLINGS.
SUN FACING,
DESERT LENGTH SPEED.
AND STAKES IN HARD GROUND.

HOPE THROAT LOCKING.
UNLIVING TO LIVE BELOW.
A HURTLING HEAT OF PASSING MASS
GOES QUIET,
GOES BY.

TURNING SIMPLE MOTIONS
GENTLE SOMBRE STRIDES.
KISS EYES UP TRUE
AND SEE SKY.
TALK TALK EVERYTHING,
BELIEVE IN THE DAY THAT COMES.

COME BACK DOWN,
THEY ALL DO,
THE CREAM LIT VOICES
OF THE DEAD.

I HEAR PURGED WORDS
MINGLED WITH MINE.
OFFERINGS OF TIME,
CIRCLING
HOLDING DOWN ON CHEST.

WE REACH, DOUBLED.
OUR ARMS LUNGING
DELAY, SWOOP, ECHO.
DISOLVE.

TELL ALL THE GHOSTS
TO COME HERE,
I WANT TO FEEL ALIVE.

COLLECTING BLOOD,
SWORN BACK IN.
EVEN CIRCLE ARMS MEET,
KNOWING IS OVER ME.
SO I LAY DOWN.

AIR SUKING SWEEPING SIGH.
THE BATH PLUG LOOSENS
AND SKIMS TO THE SIDE.
ITS ALL COMING OUT NOW.

SURFACE NAVEL
FLOATING MIDLIGHT,
WITH WIDE UNKNOWN BELOW.
DARK CUP COOLY COMFORTS,
SPRINGS TEARS
AND FOAMING CUTS.

LINES RIDE.
LIP HIGH-LOW
DESIGNING
FATES AND SEAMS
TO OPEN
TO CLOSE.

GRATEFUL WISHES RING
FOR WICKED DROUGHT
OR RAGING FLOOD.
ALL SEASONS TO FALL
AND FIND IN.

FOR NOW WAIT WINDOW,
TORSION STORMS FLY
PAST AND PASSING.
CANDLES OF TIME
I LIGHT.

SHAPES HURRY ON WALLS
AND I CALL DOWN MY
IMAGINATION TO REST
AND WISH MY HEART-GUT
A MOMENT OF PEACE,
BEFORE TAKING OFF
WITH EVERYTHING
BUNDLED LIKE HARD RUBBISH
TO BURN.

I ATTACH ALL OF MYSELF
TO ALL OF EVERY THING,
THE KINDNESS OF
PASSING LIGHTS,
OF ALL HIDING CORNERS.

LITTLE SWORD SORRY
FOR SHORT SWIMS
IN A TIDESOME WOMB.
BIRTHLESS ~~————~~
UNPROMISED ~~————~~.
UNHOMED FROM
WARM WANTING.

COMING PAST
AND WINDING
ROUND HANDLE AND JEWEL
A LIVING SIGN
ABOVE GROUND.

I SWAY AND CUT
COOL WINTER MIND.
AND KEEP YOU
WITH ME
THIS TIME.

MOUNDING MESSAGES.
TALKING CLEAR AT VOLUME
OF STOPPING EVERYTHING NOW.

EVERYTHING IN WATER,
IN WET LOVE.
ACHING LIFES CONCOCTION
FILLING VIENS HALLS.

MOTIONS CRADLE
MAKING WORTH
OF STORMS RIDE.

DRY-CRYING ON ISLANDS,
"COME SAVE US FROM
OUR BEAUTIFUL DREAM".
AS LOVE SLIPS INTO TIDES.

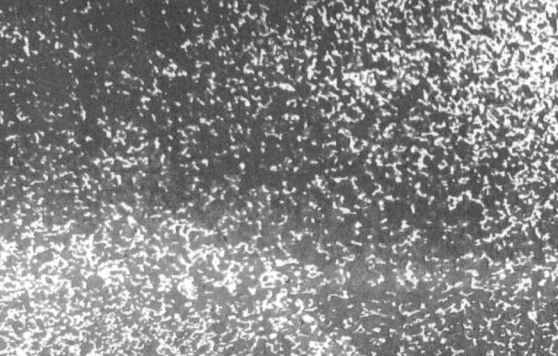

COME BY FLOATING SPIRIT.
BRING YOUR UPWARD GUST.
CALL US TO COME
TO THE SOFT WOODEN FLOOR
BEFORE THE HOUSE.

DUST DRIFTING SUN,
ADD AIR TO LIGHT,
WISH IN MOTION.
ALL CARE DYING ON
THE FRONT LAWN.

FUTURE DEATHS DORMANT.
UNHEAVING HEAVE MASS.
QUIET ALIVE
SITTING ALUMP
NEXT TO ITS DOOR.

PONDERING BEATING.
MY BLOOD
MY BLOOD.
ONE IS BEHIND
AND ONE GOES ON.

SLEEPING HARD AGAINST
BLUE WHISTLING GRAVES.
I BLINK ALONG ROADS
THAT LEAD TO MORNING.

SLEEPING BLACK WAVE
RAISING BLOOD.
I SWALLOW A LUMP HALF WAY.
~~░░░░░░░░~~

A SANE UNRAVELLING.
I GATHER, TO BARE IT.
I SQUEEZE ON AN EMPTY HAND.

ARMS RAKE IN
AND IN.
ENDLESS GATHERING
MOUNDING SWELLING GOLD.

ANKLES SNAP
OVER CLUMPING ROCK
AND SHINING HILL.

THERES NO EVEN SPACE
BUT THE RIGHT WEIGHT
IS FOUND.

CARTING AROUND
AND UPKEEPING.
BEST BE BETTER
BE BOUNDFUL BRIGHT.

UNCLIPPING,
CLIPPING BACK IN.
INSIDE OUT CARTON DRIPS.

ROLLING DOWN THE DRIVE,
BLACK PLASTIC
TO GIVE UP AND AWAY.
I CAN'T BARE THE SOUND
AS THEY PAUSE OUTSIDE
TO REMOVE
THE PIECES I LAID UNDER SKY.

SENSE SO REACHLESS
WAITING OUT THE ROOM.
ONE HOPE DELAYING ANOTHER.
WHAT CAN THERE BE
BUT TO CALL OUT.
GUESSING VOICES
SING BACK
FROM NOWHERE.

BURNING CUP
COME BACK TO ME.
I PUT MY MIND IN YOU
~~----~~ FOR KEEPING
WHILE WATER IS HIGH.

THE LIVING INSPIRED MUSCLE
SINGS WELL THERE
SURROUNDED IN FIRE.

STAY CLOSE
AS I WHISPER IN STORIES
THAT I WANT KEPT
WARM AND RAGING.

EVERY CELL OF THIS HOUSE
HAS TURNED.
I STAY HERE
UNBOLD.
I DREAM OF
SCOLDING WATER
POURED
TO MAKE LIFE HOLY.

UNKNOWN TO ME,
MASSES RISING
COVERING PLAIN AND SKY.
MOVING EARTH WEIGHT
SO CONFOUNDING
STUNNING AND PASSING
ALL FOUNDATION BELOW.

WHITE EYES LOOK LONG
THIS LIFE ROCK DEATH ROCK GROWS.
I STEP ASIDE AND ASIDE
UNTIL LIGHT IS
FULL AND TALL.

SLOW UNKNOWN
██

WIDE DISAPPERANCE.
I WANDER OFF.
I WANT OBLITERATE,
LONG ARM ORBIT,
COOL NOTHING,
LESS THAN PEACE.

PUSHING ROCKS TIGHT TOGETHER
PINCHING IN PEACE.
A MIRAGE SO SLIP-THIN
IT MUST BE
WRESTLED TO GROUND.

SOLID MOORING FEELING.
STILL AND CROUCHING
BY MY DARK.
HUNGER THIRST TRIAL.
MONTHS RINGING IN EARS.
FEET CROOKED
BELLY ROUND.
HEAD GONE,
TO LIGHTEN SHOULDERS.

TIRED AND GIVE IN
IN LOW LIGHT NIGHT.
CURLING TOWARDS SELF,
TO WILLING PIECES
SWAYING IN PASSING THOUGHT.
NEVER TRUE AT THIS
LATE HOUR,
AS GOOD CELLS
AND DEEP ROCK
HAVE SLIPPED FROM ME NOW.

OLD SHELL
I HAVE SWEAT WELL HERE.
SHARED AND PROTECTED
HOLY HOME
MADE SOFTLY.

PORTAL TO EVERYTHING HOLDING.
THE PAST ACCOMPLISHED,
SLEEPS IN SWEET PEACE
NEVER DISTURBED.
AS HEARTS PRESS
OVER IT.

MALADIES RECALLED
AND KEPT.
HOLDING TO PAINS,
DELIGHT-LIKE MIRRORS
OF AIRLESS TEARS.
KEEP THEM CLOSE
AS TIME, FORGIVELESS,
PURSUES,
THE LIGHT
THE DARK.

PASS ONE PIECE OVER.
~~XXXX~~ TAKE IT SOFT.
HERES MORE
THAT CAN BE MOVED,
STORED,
WISHED,
WILLED ON.

BRIGHT BURNT EYES CLOSE.
EVERY STEP LONG WITH
GIVING UP ATOMS,
CUPS OF JOY,
HANDFULLS OF HER.
DAYS AND DAYS WAVED OFF BY
TIMES LOVING GRIP.

POUND FOR POUNDING
COMPOUNDING SWEETNES,
MELTING AND
POURING DOWN THE THROAT.
WICKED WITH
RED BROKEN CHEEKS.
WARM WITH DIRT
PATTING DOWN ON EXISTING.

PEELING OFF BY METHOD OF
ROLLING PAST
FOR FINAL COLLECTION.
PRESSING DUST, DIRT
GRIT AND TIME
TO SKIN,
INDENTING DEARLY
ALL LESSONS
WHILE BLOOD FLOWS
QUICKLY ON RELEASE
TO FORGET THEM ALL.

THE TUNNEL.
THE LOST VERSION-YOU,
COLLABORATES
THROUGH LIGHT.
WAVING OUT REAL DREAMS,
ASKING FOR TRUST.
A COLOUR BLUE
THAT WIDENS,
FORGOTTEN AND FELT
ALL THE TIME.

HOLIDAY HEART
IN WAVE-DIP MOTION.
SWEET RISING BLUE.
SO WASHING AND KIND.
CLEAR LIMBS BELOW,
MAGNIFIED LOVELY.
I STAY IN THE WATER.

A TIRED END TO THIS.
LONG SMOKE TRAILING.
LUNGS ACCEPTING A FEW
BREATHS MORE.

BLURRY EYES RECALL
DAYS AND DAYS
OF DIRT.

I GIVE OVER
TO THE HEART BEAT
ALONGSIDE MY SPINE.

UPWARD FORWARD FLUNG.
BED TOMB MUSCLES WAKING.
I MAKE WATER,
IN PLAGUES.

I REMEMBER YOU
TO WAKING.
TO TEARS.
I SEE EVERYDAY OF YOU.
YOUR LAYING OUT,
AND LIVING.

THE CREAM LIT CLOTH SWAYING.
A HAZE OF SOULS
INHABIT THE BEDROOM CORNER.
I MAKE WATER
BUT I COME FROM DIRT.

SEPARATING WAVES.
ONE THOUGHT DYING
BESIDE ANOTHER COME LIVE.
I OPEN TO IT,
A GOLDEN GIVING IN.

WARM HANDS PASS OVER EYES.
SINKING INWARD
PAST THE DAYS GRIT,
AIDING DEEPER PIECES.
STRETCHING GLUE-LIKE SHIELDS
DOWN BELOW.
ROPE LONG RELEASING
HEAVIER AND SLOW.

EVERYTHING IS DOWN HERE
ALL DEPTHS WORTH LIVING.

CUTS INFLICTED, INFLICTING
SHARD LIKE.
WE CANT SEE THE SHAPES
FOR LAYERS OF RED DISTORT.
I LISTEN TO DEATH ON SURFACES.
FRIEND DEATH,
KISSER,
HOLDER.
QUIET DRIVER OF LIFE.

HEAT CRAVING.
SUBMERGING IN DREAMS
OF WARM WATER.
~~~~~~~~ I BECOME A STREAK,
~~~~~~ QUICK IN COMFORT.
EUPHORIC SOFT,
WITH ALL THE SALT
AND OIL MINE.

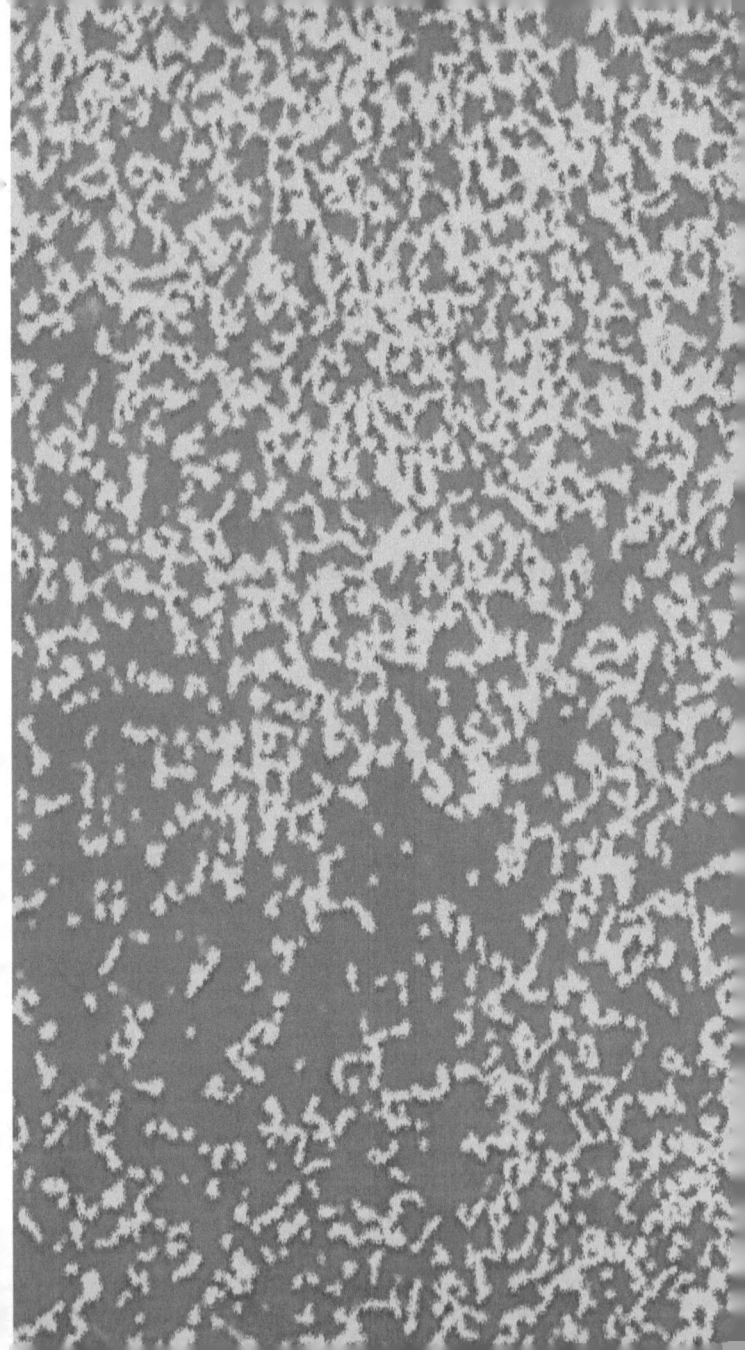